AUBURN UNIVERSITY®
COOKBOOK

MISSY MERCER

PHOTOGRAPHS BY ZAC WILLIAMS

GIBBS SMITH
TO ENRICH AND INSPIRE HUMANKIND

First Edition
15 14 13 12 11   5 4 3 2 1

Published by
Gibbs Smith
P.O. Box 667
Layton, Utah 84041

1.800.835.4993 orders
www.gibbs-smith.com

Designed by Rita Sowins/Sowins Design
Printed and bound in China

Gibbs Smith books are printed on either recycled, 100% post-consumer waste,
FSC-certified papers or on paper produced from sustainable PEFC-certified forest/
controlled wood source. Learn more at www.pefc.org.

Library of Congress Cataloging-in-Publication Data

Mercer, Missy.
  Auburn University cookbook / Missy Mercer ; photographs by Zac Williams. —
1st ed.
      p. cm.
  ISBN 978-1-4236-2148-5
  1. Cooking, American—Southern Style. 2. Cooking—Alabama—Auburn. 3.
Auburn University. 4. Cookbooks. I. Title.
  TX715.2.S68M47 2011
  641.59761'55—dc22
                              2011003604

CONTENTS

Orange-and-Blue
CARAMELIZED ONION BACON DIP

Ingredients

2 large red onions

2 tablespoons butter

1 teaspoon kosher salt

1 teaspoon cracked pepper

1/4 teaspoon cayenne pepper

4 slices maple bacon

1 package (8 ounces) cream cheese

1/2 cup Hellman's mayonnaise

1 tablespoon chopped fresh parsley

Crackers, of choice

✳ Serves 8–10 ✳

Slice onions into thin half moons. Over medium heat, melt butter and sauté onions with salt, pepper, and cayenne in a large non-stick frying pan, uncovered, for 30–45 minutes.

While the onions are cooking, place bacon in separate pan and cook until crisp. Cool and then crumble. In a large bowl, combine the cream cheese and mayonnaise. Add onions and bacon; mix to combine. Top with parsley for garnish and serve with crackers.

Rah Rah Rah!
CORN AND AVOCADO SALSA

Ingredients

4 ears of corn

1/2 red bell pepper, diced

1/2 red onion, diced

2 tomatoes, peeled, seeded, and diced

3 tablespoons chopped fresh cilantro

1 bunch green onions, chopped

2 cloves garlic, chopped

2 ripe avocados, diced

1/2 cup apple cider vinegar

1 cup extra virgin olive oil

1 tablespoon lime juice

2 teaspoons cumin

2 teaspoons chipotle chile powder

Salt and pepper, to taste

Cholula Hot Sauce

Tortilla chips

Preheat oven to 400 degrees. Slice corn off cob and spread kernels on a greased baking sheet with sides. Place in oven and roast for 30 minutes. Remove from oven and cool. Gently toss corn and bell pepper, red onion, tomatoes, cilantro, green onions, garlic, and avocados in a large bowl.

In a large cruet or medium bowl, combine vinegar, oil, lime juice, cumin, and chile powder. Pour over vegetables and lightly stir to combine. Season with salt, pepper, and hot sauce. Serve with tortilla chips.

✳ Serves 8–10 ✳

The Tiger Walk™
SPINACH–ARTICHOKE DIP

Ingredients

2 packages (10 ounces each) frozen chopped spinach

2 tablespoons butter

2 tablespoons flour

$^1/_2$ cup evaporated milk

8 ounces pepper jack cheese

$^1/_2$ teaspoon cracked pepper

$^1/_2$ teaspoon granulated garlic

1 teaspoon salt

$^1/_2$ teaspoon Worcestershire sauce

1 can (8 ounces) artichoke hearts

Grated Parmesan cheese

Crackers, of choice

✽ Serves 8–10 ✽

Preheat oven 350 degrees. Cook spinach according to package directions and reserve $^1/_2$ cup cooking liquid.

In a large saucepan, melt butter and add flour, stirring constantly. Add milk and reserved liquid and cook until it thickens. Add pepper jack cheese, pepper, garlic, salt, and Worcestershire sauce, stirring to combine. Fold in spinach and artichoke hearts.

Place in a 9 x 9-inch buttered casserole dish, sprinkle with Parmesan cheese and bake until it bubbles, approximately 30–45 minutes. Serve with crackers.

Variation: If you would like to offer dip as individual servings, bake as directed and then scoop into 8–10 ramekins or small decorative bowls and serve.

Go Big Blue
HOT WING DIP

Ingredients

8 ounces cream cheese

1 jar (16 ounces) chunky blue cheese dressing

3 cups shredded chicken

1 package (8 ounces) crumbled blue cheese

2 tablespoons melted butter

1/2 cup Crystal Hot Wing Sauce, or hot sauce of choice

Corn chips

✳ Serves 8–10 ✳

Preheat oven to 350 degrees. In a large bowl, combine cream cheese and half of the dressing; mix in chicken. Place in 9 x 9-inch buttered casserole dish. Sprinkle blue cheese over the chicken mixture and then spoon on remaining dressing. Combine butter and hot sauce then pour over dip. Bake for 30 minutes or until cheese bubbles. Let cool slightly before serving. Serve with corn chips.

Variation: If you would like to offer dip as individual servings, bake as directed and then scoop into 8–10 ramekins or small decorative bowls and serve.

Roasted Red
BEAT-THE-TIDE HUMMUS

Ingredients

1 red bell pepper, roasted,
   peeled, and seeded

2 tablespoons water

8 cloves garlic

$1/2$ cup tahini paste

Juice of 1 lemon

2 cans (12 ounces each)
   garbanzo beans,
   drained and rinsed

Extra virgin olive oil

Salt and cracked
   pepper, to taste

Artisan bread or pita chips

✳ Serves 8–10 ✳

Using a food processor, purée bell pepper with water
and set aside. Process the garlic, tahini, and lemon
juice until it forms a paste. Add garbanzo beans,
and slowly add oil until the desired consistency is
achieved. Mix in bell pepper and season with salt
and pepper. Serve with bread or pita chips.

AU® Spicy
QUESO DIP

Ingredients

2 pounds Velveeta cheese, chunked

3 cloves garlic, minced

$^1/_2$ jar (4 ounces) pimentos, diced

1 jalapeño, seeded and chopped

$^1/_2$ jar smoked tomato salsa

Salt and pepper, to taste

Tabasco sauce, to taste

Tortilla chips

✳ Serves 8–10 ✳

In a double boiler or crock pot, combine cheese, garlic, pimentos, and jalapeño and melt. Stir in salsa then season with salt, pepper and Tabasco. Serve with tortilla chips.

Tailgater's
PARTY MIX

Ingredients

1/4 cup butter

3 teaspoons seasoned salt

2 tablespoons
Worcestershire sauce

2 cups Cheerios

2 cups Corn Chex

2 cups Wheat Chex

2 cups Rice Chex

1 1/2 cups pretzel sticks

2 cups cheddar gold fish

2 cups mixed nuts

✳ Serves 15–20 ✳

Preheat oven to 250 degrees. Melt butter in large roasting pan and add salt and Worcestershire sauce. Stir in all cereals, pretzel sticks, gold fish, and nuts until coated. Bake for at least 1 hour, stirring every 15 minutes, and then spread on paper towels to cool. The mix will keep for two weeks in ziplock bags or airtight containers.

Go Tigers!

Cheese Biscuit
TIGER BITES

Ingredients

2 cups flour

$1/2$ teaspoon salt

3 teaspoons baking powder

4 tablespoons Crisco

$2/3$ cup grated cheddar cheese

$2/3$ cup milk

1 pound Conecuh Cajun smoked sausage

✳ Makes 24 bites ✳

Preheat oven to 425 degrees. In a large bowl, sift together flour, salt, and baking powder. Using a pastry cutter or fork, cut Crisco into flour mixture until it has a crumbly appearance. Add cheddar cheese and stir to combine. Add milk and mix until dough forms. Roll dough out on a floured surface and cut 24 small biscuits with a biscuit cutter. Using the rolling pin, flatten the biscuits just a bit.

Slice the sausage into twelve 1-inch pieces and then cut in half. Place a sausage piece in the middle of each biscuit, fold up the sides of the dough, and pinch at the top to make a little pocket. Place on a parchment-lined baking sheet and bake for 10–15 minutes until golden brown. Serve while hot or at room temperature.

Sis Boom Bah!
SAUSAGE BALLS

Ingredients

1 pound extra sharp cheddar cheese, grated

3 cups Bisquick

6 tablespoons corn meal

1 pound Jimmy Dean Hot Sausage

1/2 teaspoon red chili powder

* Makes approximately 4 dozen balls *

Preheat oven to 375 degrees. In a large bowl, thoroughly combine all ingredients and roll into 1-inch balls. Place on a baking sheet and bake 15–20 minutes or until browned on the outside.

Aubie's™
HAM-AND-CHEESE PUFFS

Ingredients

- $^1/_2$ **cup butter, room temperature**
- $1^1/_2$ **cups grated extra sharp cheddar cheese**
- $^1/_2$ **cup finely-chopped honey-baked ham**
- $^1/_4$ **teaspoon Worcestershire sauce**
- **Pinch cayenne pepper**
- **1 cup flour**

✳ Serves 8–10 ✳

Preheat oven to 350 degrees. In a large bowl, thoroughly combine all ingredients. Roll into 1-inch balls and place on parchment-lined baking sheet. Bake for 15–20 minutes or until lightly browned.

Weegle Weegle™
CHICKEN SALAD POCKETS

Ingredients

2 packages (3 ounces each) cream cheese

6 tablespoons butter, melted and divided

4 cups cubed cooked chicken

1/2 teaspoon salt

1/4 teaspoon pepper

4 tablespoons milk

2 tablespoons chopped green onions

2 tablespoons pecan pieces

2 packages (10 ounces each) Big and Flaky Pillsbury Crescent Rolls

1 1/2 cups Parmesan bread crumbs

✳ Makes 12 ✳

Preheat oven to 350 degrees. In a large bowl, blend cream cheese and 4 tablespoons butter until smooth. Add in next 6 ingredients.

Separate crescent rolls along perforations and spoon 1/2 cup chicken mixture into the center of each triangle. Pull sides up, slightly twist, and pinch together like a pouch. Brush tops with remaining butter and sprinkle with bread crumbs. Place on baking sheet and bake for 20–30 minutes or until browned and rolls are done.

24

Roll Over the Tide CHICKEN WINGS

Ingredients

Juice of 1 orange

Juice of 2 lemons

2 cloves garlic, minced

1 tablespoon brown sugar

1/4 cup olive oil

1 teaspoon salt

2 teaspoons Chipotle en Adobo, puréed

3 pounds chicken wings

2 cups mixed nuts

2 cups breadcrumbs

✱ Serves 8 ✱

In a small bowl, combine juices, garlic, brown sugar, oil, salt, and chipotle purée. Place chicken wings in a large ziplock bag, add marinade, and let rest for at least 2 hours at room temperature. Refrigerate if you don't plan on cooking right away.

Preheat oven to 450 degrees. In a food processor, pulse mixed nuts until finely ground, taking care not to turn into nut butter, and then combine with breadcrumbs in a large bowl. Toss chicken in nut mixture. Place in foiled-lined 9 x 13–inch baking dish and bake for 30 minutes. Turn over the chicken wings and bake another 30 minutes. Cover with aluminum foil halfway through baking if the wings get too dark on the outside.

Orange-and-Blue
MARINATED PORK TENDERLOIN

Ingredients

1 cup soy sauce

$1/2$ cup honey

$1/4$ cup orange juice

2 tablespoons black
  bean sauce

4 garlic cloves, crushed

1 tablespoon grated
  fresh ginger

4 green onions, chopped

1 tablespoon dry mustard

$2^{1}/2$ to 3 pounds
  pork tenderloin
  (approximately 2 loins)

✳ Serves 10 ✳

Combine first 8 ingredients in a large bowl, add tenderloins, and marinate for at least 8 hours in the refrigerator.

Preheat oven to 350 degrees. Remove tenderloin from marinade and place in roasting pan with a rack. Cook for approximately 50 minutes or until internal temperature reaches 170 degrees. Let cool completely and refrigerate overnight. When ready to serve, slice in $1/4$-inch thick slices and place on a serving platter.

Flank Steak
"SLIDER INTO THE END ZONE"

Ingredients

1½ pounds flank steak

½ cup olive oil

½ cup tamari or low sodium soy sauce

4 garlic cloves, minced

1 loaf of artisan bread, preferably long and round, thinly sliced

Optional toppings: Jezebel Sauce (recipe to follow), caramelized red onions, smoked Swiss cheese, or sautéed mushrooms

Score flank steak on both sides. Place in a long shallow pan. In a small bowl, mix oil, tamari, and garlic together. Pour over flank steak and let marinate for at least 6 hours in the refrigerator. Turn every hour during the process.

Preheat broiler or grill. Remove steak from the marinade, place on broiler pan, and broil approximately 5 minutes on each side on the top shelf of the oven closest to the broiler. Let meat cool, then slice on diagonal and place on toasted bread rounds with desired toppings, or make mini sandwiches.

✳ Serves 10 ✳

Jezebel Sauce Ingredients

1 jar (16 ounces) pineapple marmalade

1 jar (16 ounces) apple jelly

2 tablespoons dry mustard

½ jar (5 ounces) horseradish

In a small saucepan, heat all ingredients until jelly is melted and everything is thoroughly combined. Serve at room temperature. Flavors intensify after a couple days, so make two days or so before you want to serve it. Store in refrigerator.

✳ Makes 4 cups ✳

Tiger
ROAST BEEF PINWHEELS

Ingredients

8 ounces chive-flavored cream cheese

1 package (8-inch) flour tortillas

1 pound shaved roast beef

16 leaves green leaf lettuce

Dip, of choice

✳ Serves 8–10 ✳

Spread cream cheese on one side of each tortilla and layer with roast beef then lettuce. Roll tightly and individually wrap each tortilla in plastic wrap. Refrigerate for at least 2 hours. When ready to serve, slice in $1/4$-inch rounds as appetizers or in half for wraps. Place on platter and serve with dip of choice.

Kick 'em in the Butt
Big Blue
CHILI

Ingredients

1 pound ground beef

1 can (15 ounces) tomato sauce

1 can (15 ounces) stewed tomatoes

1 can (15 ounces) red kidney beans, rinsed and drained

1 can (15 ounces) white beans, rinsed and drained

1 can (15 ounces) pinto beans, rinsed and drained

1 tablespoon lime juice

1 tablespoon chili powder

2 teaspoons salt

2 teaspoons cilantro

2 teaspoons cumin

2 teaspoons paprika

Grated cheddar cheese

Tortilla or corn chips

Brown ground beef in large stock pot. Add tomatoes, beans, and seasonings. Bring to a boil then simmer for 2 hours. Adjust seasonings to taste. Serve with cheese and chips.

✳ Serves 10 ✳

Halftime
DOUBLE-DIPPED
FRIED CHICKEN

Ingredients

4 cups buttermilk

$1/2$ tablespoon dried thyme

2 tablespoons Tabasco sauce

2 tablespoons Worcestershire sauce

2 tablespoons kosher salt, divided

$3^1/2$ teaspoons cracked pepper, divided

2 whole fryer chickens, cut into pieces

3 cups flour

1 tablespoon Cajun seasoning

Cooking oil

✳ Serves 8 ✳

In a large bowl, combine first 4 ingredients with 1 tablespoon salt and $1^1/2$ teaspoons of pepper. Add chicken and marinate overnight in the refrigerator.

Remove chicken from refrigerator at least 1 hour before frying. In a large bowl, combine flour, Cajun seasoning, and remaining salt and pepper. Remove chicken from buttermilk marinade; dip in seasoned flour, then in buttermilk, then again in the flour for a final dip. Fry at 375 degrees until internal temperature of chicken reaches 180 degrees. This chicken is divine warm, but it is also wonderful cold the next day.

Auburn®
MARINATED
POTATO SALAD

Ingredients

12 small red new potatoes

7 to 8 stalks celery, diced

1 bunch green onions, chopped

1/2 cup chopped fresh parsley

2 tablespoons chopped fresh basil

1/2 cup white wine

1/4 cup apple cider vinegar

1/2 cup extra virgin olive oil

4 cloves garlic, minced

2 teaspoons seasoned salt

Cracked pepper, to taste

* Serves 8-10 *

In a medium stock pot, cover whole potatoes with water and boil just until a fork can pierce but not break the potatoes apart. Drain and cool.

Slice potatoes in 1/2-inch pieces and combine with celery, onions, parsley, and basil in a large bowl. Mix white wine, vinegar, oil, garlic, and seasonings together in a small bowl to make a dressing. Combine dressing with vegetables and serve at room temperature or slightly chilled.

War Eagle® Hey!
SWEET-AND-SOUR COLESLAW

Ingredients

1 head green cabbage, shredded

1 cup sugar

1 tablespoon plus 1 teaspoon kosher salt

2 large carrots, grated

$1/2$ teaspoon celery seed

$3/4$ cup extra virgin olive oil

$1/2$ cup apple cider vinegar

Cracked pepper, to taste

✱ Serves 8-10 ✱

Combine cabbage, sugar, and salt in a colander and let sit for at least 1 hour. Drain any liquid that remains in colander. Place cabbage, carrots, celery seed, oil, and vinegar into a large bowl then toss. Season with pepper. Cover and refrigerate until ready to serve.

Touchdown
BOURBON-BAKED BEANS

Ingredients

- **1/2 pound Jimmy Dean Hot Bulk Sausage**
- **3 cans (16 ounces each) red kidney beans, rinsed and drained**
- **1/2 medium red onion, diced**
- **1 jar (18 ounces) Sweet Baby Ray's Sweet Vidalia Onion Barbecue Sauce***
- **1 heaping tablespoon Dijon mustard**
- **1/4 cup bourbon**

✱ Serves 8–10 ✱

Preheat oven to 350 degrees. Cook sausage in a medium frying pan, stirring to break up into crumbles. Drain fat and then combine with remaining ingredients in a large bowl. Place in a 9 x 13-inch casserole dish, cover with aluminum foil, and bake for 30 minutes or until mixture bubbles.

*Other sauces may be substituted, but the sweetness of this particular sauce is the key to the flavor.

Greek
PASTA SALAD

Ingredients

1 small box orzo pasta

1 cup thinly sliced salami

1 cup sliced black olives

2 tablespoons capers

**1 cup thinly sliced
   spinach leaves**

1¹/₂ cup crumbled feta

Zest from 1 lemon

1 cup Italian dressing

✳ Serves 10–12 ✳

Cook pasta as directed on box, drain, and cool
completely. In a large bowl, toss pasta with all other
ingredients. Cool completely before serving.

Aubie's™
HEART-OF-DIXIE CAVIAR

Ingredients

1 Vidalia onion, chopped

2 jalapeño peppers, seeded and minced

1 green bell pepper, finely chopped

1 bunch green onions, chopped

4 garlic cloves, minced

2 medium tomatoes, diced

2 cups corn

2 cans (15.8 ounces each) black-eyed peas

1 cup Italian dressing

1/4 cup fresh cilantro, chopped

Sour cream, optional

Tortilla chips

In a large bowl, combine first 9 ingredients and let chill overnight. Drain and then stir in cilantro. Place in serving bowl and top with sour cream, if you like. Serve with tortilla chips.

✱ Serves 15–20 ✱

Fourth Quarter
WHISKEY SLUSH

Ingredients

2 cups unsweetened black tea

5 cups water

**2 cups Jack Daniel's
Black Label whiskey**

¼ cup sugar

**1 can (12 ounces)
frozen lemonade
concentrate, thawed**

**1 can (6 ounces)
frozen orange juice
concentrate, thawed**

Ginger ale

✳ Serves 6–8 ✳

In a large pitcher, combine tea, water, whiskey, sugar, and juices. Pour into an 11 x 14-inch pan and place in the freezer. Stir with a fork every hour until the mixture has the consistency of a slushy. This will take about 2 hours. Spoon slush into 12-ounce glasses, filling three-fourths full, and top with ginger ale.

Orange-and-Blue
PASSION

Ingredients

1 cup orange juice

1 cup ginger ale

¹/₂ cup orange-flavored Stoli vodka

Ice cubes

Blue Curaco

* Serves 2 *

In a blender, blend orange juice, ginger ale, and vodka with enough ice cubes to make it slightly slushy. Pour into chilled 12-ounce glasses and top with a shot of Blue Curaco poured over each drink to finish.

Kick it Big Blue
PUNCH

Ingredients

2 cups sugar

4 cups water

1 pint Patron Tequila

2 ounces Grand Marnier

2 cups Simply Limeade

3 tablespoons orange extract

✻ Serves 6-8 ✻

Combine the sugar and water in a large saucepan and boil until the sugar is dissolved. Let cool and combine with remaining ingredients in a large pitcher. Chill until ready to serve. Serve over ice.

Tiger Paw
COOKIES

Ingredients

2 sticks butter, softened

$3/4$ cup sugar

3 egg yolks

$2^1/2$ cups flour

1 teaspoon baking powder

$1/2$ teaspoon salt

Royal Icing

4 cups powdered sugar

3 tablespoons meringue powder*

$2/3$ cup water

Orange and blue food coloring

✱ Makes 2–3 dozen cookies depending on the size of the cookie cutter ✱

Preheat oven to 400 degrees. In a large bowl, beat butter and sugar together until light and fluffy using an electric mixer. Beat in egg yolks one at a time. Add flour, baking powder, and salt; mix on low until incorporated. Refrigerate dough for at least 1 hour.

Working with half of the dough at a time, roll out to $1/8$- to $1/4$-inch thickness on a lightly floured surface. Cut out paw print-shaped cookies with a cutter and place on parchment-lined baking sheets. Bake for 6–10 minutes or until lightly browned on edges. Remove to cooling racks.

Combine sugar and meringue powder in mixer with paddle attachment. Slowly add water and mix until the sugar has dissolved and the mixture becomes a thick glossy paste, about 5–7 minutes. Adjust the consistency by adding either more powdered sugar for thickness or water to thin. Spread a layer of white icing on cookies and then unequally divide the remaining icing into 2 bowls. Tint the larger amount orange and the other blue and then decorate cookies.

*Meringue powder is sold in grocery stores as powdered egg whites.

Miss Ruth's
COOKIES

Ingredients

1 cup sugar

1 cup brown sugar

2 sticks butter, softened

1 cup vegetable oil

1 egg

1 teaspoon vanilla

1 teaspoon cream of tartar

1 teaspoon baking soda

3$\frac{1}{2}$ cups flour

1 cup Rice Krispies

1 cup coconut

1 cup rolled oats

$\frac{1}{2}$ cup pecan pieces

✳ Makes 4–5 dozen cookies ✳

Preheat oven to 350 degrees. Combine first 4 ingredients in a large bowl. Add egg and vanilla. In another large bowl, combine cream of tartar, baking soda, and flour. Stir flour mixture into sugar mixture. Add Rice Krispies, coconut, oats, and pecans. Combine thoroughly then drop by large spoonfuls onto baking sheet lined with parchment paper. Press down with a fork and bake for approximately 15 minutes.

Old South
WHITE CHOCOLATE PECAN BLONDIES

Ingredients

1 cup butter

1 pound white chocolate, half chunked and half chopped

4 eggs

1 cup sugar

1 teaspoon vanilla

1 pinch salt

2 cups flour

$1/3$ cup pecan pieces

8 ounces semisweet chocolate chips

✳ Makes 12 large or 24 small blondies ✳

Preheat oven to 300 degrees. Line an 11 x 14-inch pan with parchment paper. In a medium bowl over a hot water bath, combine butter with chunks of white chocolate. In a large bowl, whisk eggs, sugar, vanilla, and salt. Add chocolate mixture to egg mixture and stir in flour. When cooled slightly, add chopped white chocolate, pecans, and chocolate chips. Pour into prepared pan. Bake for 30–40 minutes or until skewer or toothpick comes out clean when tested.

The Tiger's Den
LEMON BARS

Ingredients

2¼ cups flour, divided

½ cup powdered sugar

**¾ cup butter, chilled and
cut into small pieces**

4 eggs

1½ cup sugar

2 tablespoons lemon zest

½ cup lemon juice

1 teaspoon baking powder

¼ teaspoon salt

✱ Makes 12 large or
24 small bars ✱

Preheat oven to 325 degrees. In a medium bowl, combine 2 cups flour and powdered sugar. Using a pastry cutter, cut butter into mixture until crumbly. Press into a 9 x 13-inch pan lined with parchment paper and bake for 10–15 minutes or until lightly browned. In a large bowl, whisk together eggs, sugar, zest, and juice. In a small bowl, combine baking powder, salt, and remaining flour; combine with egg mixture. Pour into prepared crust and bake for 30–40 minutes or until filling is set. Cool completely and slice into bars. Sprinkle with sifted powdered sugar before serving.

War Damn . . .
THAT'S GOOD
BANANA PUDDING!

Ingredients

2 cups sugar

6 tablespoons cornstarch

¼ teaspoon salt

6 cups whole milk

7 egg yolks

6 tablespoons butter, diced

1 tablespoon vanilla

6 large bananas, thinly sliced

**1 box (12 ounces)
  vanilla wafers**

✳ Serves 8–10 ✳

To make the custard; combine sugar, cornstarch, salt, and eggs in a large bowl. Place milk in a large saucepan and bring to a boil. Very slowly add warm milk to egg mixture. Whisk together and place back in pan over medium heat and cook, stirring constantly, until thickened. Strain into a large bowl and add butter and vanilla. Cover with plastic wrap directly placed on surface of custard and chill.

When custard is cool, assemble the pudding. Place a layer of vanilla wafers in 9 x 14-inch baking pan and top with layer of thinly sliced bananas. Top with custard then another layer of banana slices and vanilla wafers. Chill until ready to eat.

Variation: You can also assemble the pudding as individual servings by using dessert bowls or even glasses as shown.

MISSY MERCER was born and raised in the Deep South. Her Italian background and frequent visits with her grandmother inspired her to pursue her dream of opening a restaurant. She graduated from Auburn University with a degree in finance and then attended the California Culinary Academy in San Francisco. She has over fifteen years of experience in the restaurant business as well as teaching cooking classes and working in a test kitchen. Missy and her husband, Browne, jointly own two restaurants and a bakery in the Old Cloverdale district of Montgomery, Alabama.